EGYPTIAN MUMMIES

by Tyler Gieseke

abdobooks.com

Published by Pop!, a division of ABDO, PO Box 398166, Minneapolis, Minnesota 55439. Copyright ©2022 by Abdo Consulting Group, Inc. International copyrights reserved in all countries. No part of this book may be reproduced in any form without written permission from the publisher. DiscoverRoo™ is a trademark and logo of Pop!.

Printed in the United States of America, North Mankato, Minnesota.

052021
092021

THIS BOOK CONTAINS RECYCLED MATERIALS

Cover Photos: Shutterstock Images

Interior Photos: Shutterstock Images, 1, 6, 10–11, 13, 14–15, 16–17, 28–29; icona/Alamy, 5; New York Public Library Digital Collections, 7; Mohamed El Raai/picture-alliance/dpa/AP Images, 9; iStockphoto, 19; Associated Press, 20, 22–23; Sun_Shine/Shutterstock.com, 21; Mirko Kuzmanovic/Shutterstock.com, 25; Peter Steffen/picture-alliance/dpa/AP Images, 26–27

Editor: Elizabeth Andrews
Series Designer: Laura Graphenteen

Library of Congress Control Number: 2020921107

Publisher's Cataloging-in-Publication Data

Names: Gieseke, Tyler, author.

Title: Egyptian mummies / by Tyler Gieseke

Description: Minneapolis, Minnesota : Pop!, 2022 | Series: Ancient Egypt | Includes online resources and index.

Identifiers: ISBN 9781532169878 (lib. bdg.) | ISBN 9781644945346 (pbk.) | ISBN 9781098240806 (ebook)

Subjects: LCSH: Mummies--Egypt--Juvenile literature. | Egypt--Antiquities--Juvenile literature. | Funeral rites and ceremonies--Egypt--Juvenile literature. | Egypt--History--Juvenile literature. | Africa--Religious life and customs--Juvenile literature.

Classification: DDC 932.01--dc23

WELCOME TO DiscoverRoo!

Pop open this book and you'll find QR codes loaded with information, so you can learn even more!

Scan this code* and others like it while you read, or visit the website below to make this book pop!

popbooksonline.com/egyptian-mummies

*Scanning QR codes requires a web-enabled smart device with a QR code reader app and a camera.

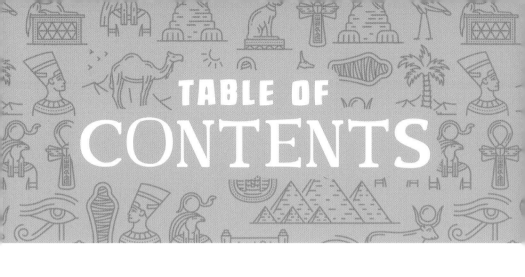

TABLE OF CONTENTS

CHAPTER 1
What is a Mummy?. 4

CHAPTER 2
The Mummy Method 10

CHAPTER 3
Famous Mummies. 18

CHAPTER 4
Studying the Dead. 24

Making Connections. 30
Glossary 31
Index. 32
Online Resources 32

WHAT IS A MUMMY?

A girl explores a museum with her family. She looks at displays about ancient Egypt. The girl enjoys learning about ancient societies.

WATCH A VIDEO HERE!

Visitors can see ancient Egyptian mummies in museums around the world.

She sees a human shape covered in thin strips of cloth. "What is that?" she wonders. It is a mummy!

Bodies of people and animals normally decay in a few months after death.

A mummy is a dead body that is prepared so it doesn't **decay** like normal. This way the body can be in good condition for many years. Sometimes, mummies are **preserved** for several thousand years.

DID YOU KNOW?

Scientists found a mummy in Egypt that was more than 5,000 years old!

Several societies have created mummies throughout history. But the mummies of ancient Egypt are the most well known. Ancient Egyptians believed turning a person's body into a mummy would help the person's soul in the afterlife.

Scientists have discovered and continue to find

NATURAL MUMMIES

Not all mummies are made by humans. Sometimes, nature turns bodies into mummies that last many years. A body that is stuck in ice and snow can become a mummy. People also find natural mummies in places that are hot and dry, like deserts.

Scientists discovered this Egyptian burial room in 2018.

mummies in ancient Egyptian **tombs**.

They use technology to study the

mummies. They learn about their lives.

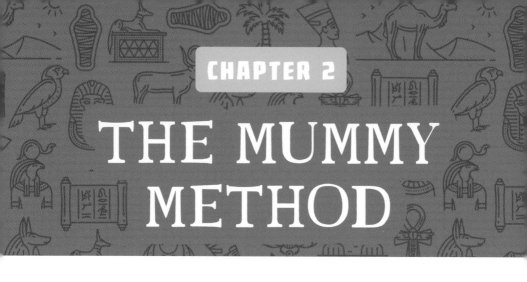

THE MUMMY METHOD

In ancient Egypt, making a mummy took a long time. The method to create a mummy was called embalming.

COMPLETE AN ACTIVITY HERE!

Embalming the bodies of kings and nobles took about 70 days. The embalmers were often priests.

Anubis was the god of mummies. He had the head of a jackal.

First, the embalmer washed the body and covered it in scented oils. Then the embalmer took out the stomach and other guts. Next, the embalmer used a hook to take the brain out through the nose.

The heart remained in the body. Egyptians believed it was the root of life. They thought the heart was important in the **afterlife**.

DID YOU KNOW?

Egyptians believed gods and goddesses weighed people's hearts after death. A heavy heart meant the person did wrong in life.

The jars had the heads of the god Horus's four sons.

Then, the embalmer placed the guts in jars to dry. The embalmer also filled and covered the body with salts to dry it. The body sat for 40 days.

After the body dried, the embalmer removed the salts and refilled the body with spices. The embalmer wrapped the guts in cloth. They went back inside the mummy. Magic **amulets** sometimes went in too.

Ancient Egyptians greatly honored the method of making a mummy.

The embalmer wrapped the mummy in strips of cloth, starting at the head. Finally, people put the completed mummy in a **sarcophagus**. Then it went inside a **tomb**.

DID YOU KNOW?

Sometimes, ancient Egyptians embalmed cats. They believed all cats were blessed.

Ankh

- Meant endless life
- Many drawings showed goddesses and gods holding ankhs.

Eye of Horus

- Meant protection and healing
- Egyptians believed the **pharaoh** was really the god Horus in human form.

AMAZING AMULETS

Ancient Egyptians often buried mummies with amulets in the cloth wrappings. Amulets gave magical protection or other benefits. Egyptians often made them from a special clay.

Scarab beetle

- Meant rebirth and new life
- Scarab beetles are winged insects.

Lotus flower

- Meant creation and rebirth
- Lotus flowers sink into the water at night. Then they rise to the surface during the day.

CHAPTER 3

FAMOUS MUMMIES

Some ancient Egyptian mummies are famous because they were rulers when they were alive. Some are famous because they came from grand **tombs**. Wealthy people could afford these tombs.

LEARN MORE HERE!

In 1881 CE,

archaeologists found

the mummy of Ramses II.

He was a **pharaoh**. His

mummy was in a burial

place called the Valley

of the Kings. Now, visitors

can see Ramses at the

Egyptian Museum

in Cairo, Egypt.

Ramses II ruled for 66 years.

Visitors of the museum can also see Hatshepsut's mummy. She was the pharaoh for more than 20 years. Hatshepsut died in 1458 BCE. She was one of just a few female pharaohs!

Archaeologists found the mummy of Hatshepsut in a tomb in the Valley of the Kings.

The Egyptian Museum in Cairo opened in 1858 CE.

Scientists carefully move King Tut's mummy.

Archaeologist Howard Carter discovered the mummy of Tutankhamon, or King Tut. He found the mummy in 1922 CE. King Tut is known for his decorated **sarcophagus**. Tut's mummy is on display in the Valley of the Kings.

DID YOU KNOW?

King Tut became pharaoh when he was only nine years old.

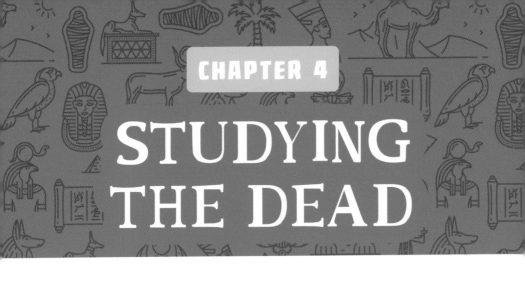

Archaeologists are still discovering and studying mummies today. They use advanced technology. This teaches them about the mummies and how ancient Egyptians lived.

LEARN MORE HERE!

In 2018, archaeologists found a room where ancient embalmers made mummies. It was in a burial place called Saqqara.

The room had areas arranged for different steps in the embalming method. Four very old **sarcophagi** were also there. They had mummies inside!

Technology like X-ray machines can give more information about mummies. An educator at a university in Chicago studied the mummy of a young girl. He used X-ray pictures. The pictures showed him that the girl didn't die from a wound. He believes she died from an illness.

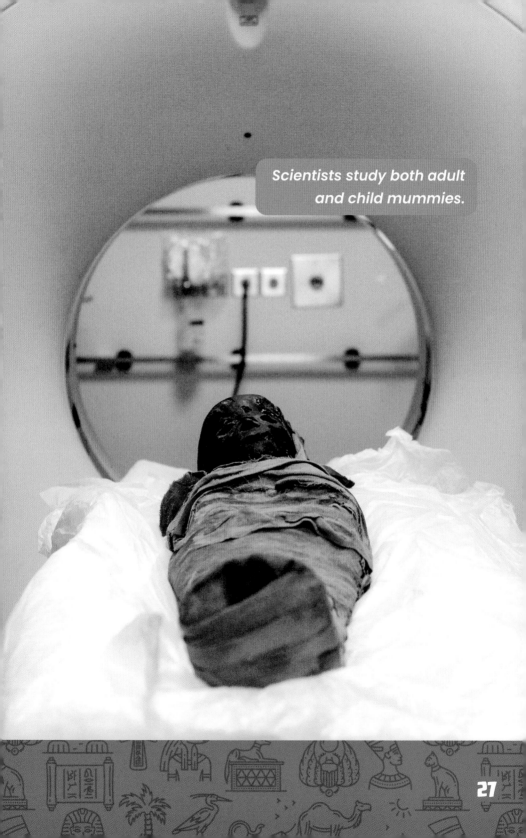

Scientists study both adult and child mummies.

WRAPPING A MUMMY

1

2

Embalmers used salts to dry a body.

3

The mummy was wrapped in layers of cloth.

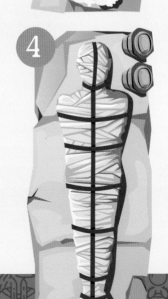

4

Egyptian mummies are important remains. They let people look back in time at one ancient society. People will learn from mummies for a long time.

5

A finished mummy went in a decorated sarcophagus.

MAKING CONNECTIONS

TEXT-TO-SELF

Have you seen a mummy in a museum before? If so, what did you think of it? If not, would you like to? Why or why not?

TEXT-TO-TEXT

Have you read about how other societies treat their dead? How do those ideas compare with what you read in this book?

TEXT-TO-WORLD

How should scientists handle mummies and the things in their tombs? Do they need to be respectful? Why or why not?

GLOSSARY

afterlife — life that exists after physical death.

amulet — a small item or sign that people wear for magical effects.

archaeologist — a scientist who studies past human societies through the things left behind.

decay — to break down, especially after death.

pharaoh — the highest ruler in ancient Egypt.

preserve — to keep something in good condition.

sarcophagus — a large container for a dead body, often decorated and made of stone.

tomb — a place where people bury or put their dead, usually to honor them.

INDEX

afterlife, 8, 12

archaeologist, 8–9, 19, 23–25

Cairo, 19

Carter, Howard, 23

embalming, 10–15, 25

Hatshepsut, 20

King Tut, 23

Ramses II, 19

Saqqara, 25

Valley of the Kings, 19, 23

ONLINE RESOURCES
popbooksonline.com

Scan this code* and others like it while you read, or visit the website below to make this book pop!

popbooksonline.com/egyptian-mummies

*Scanning QR codes requires a web-enabled smart device with a QR code reader app and a camera.